ANTIQUE HUMOUR

by
JOEL ROTHMAN

Cartoons by
CHIC JACOB

GW00601129

Robson Books

Other cartoon books by Joel Rothman

ADULTERY CAN BE FUNNY
SMOKERS' HUMOUR
THE CANNIBAL COOKBOOK
THE LAST MEOW
POLITICS IS A FUNNY BUSINESS
BOOZE WHO

FIRST PUBLISHED IN GREAT BRITAIN IN 1983 BY
ROBSON BOOKS LTD., BOLSOVER HOUSE,
5-6 CLIPSTONE STREET, LONDON W1P 7EB.
COPYRIGHT © 1983 J.R. PUBLICATIONS INC.

British Library Cataloguing in Publication Data

Antique humour.
   1. Antiques—Anecdotes, facetiae, satire, etc.
   I. Rothman, Joel
   745.PO75   NK1125

   ISBN 0-86051-238-X

Printed in Hungary

There are only three kinds of furniture — antique, modern, and comfortable.

Many people buy antique furniture on the instalment plan. The furniture is new when they buy it, but antique by the time it's paid for.

Antique chair — something that cost £5 to make, £500 to buy, and £1,000 to restore.

★　★　★

The family antiques which have been handed down from generation to generation prove beyond a doubt that the children of your ancestors were better behaved than your own.

A man had been unemployed for many months, but at last he found work in an antique emporium. On his very first day he knocked over a lamp.

"That's a very expensive antique you've just broken," said the manager. "You'll have to pay for it. The cost will be deducted every week from your salary."

"How much will that come to?" asked the newly em-employed man.

"Three thousand pounds."

"Great — at last I've got a steady job!"

A newlywed consulted a home decorator for advice on the best way to fix up her flat.

"What type of furniture do you have?" asked the decorator. "Modern, French, Provincial, Chippendale?"

"You might call it Early Matrimonial," explained the young bride. "Some of it is his mother's and some of it is my mother's."

A man was looking at a table in an antique shop.

"How old is this table?" he asked the assistant.

"It's 304 years."

"How can you be so exact?" asked the man.

"Well," replied the assistant, "the owner told me it was 300 years old, and that was when I first started working here — four years ago."

Once there was a man who bought all his clothes and furniture secondhand. By constant thrift he was able to send his daughter to college. The daughter graduated and became a wealthy lawyer, while the father continued his frugality. "I just heard from my daughter," he told his friend. "She went to Paris and paid £100,000 for some chairs that belonged to Louis XIV."

"Really?" said the friend. "So you've taught her to buy secondhand, too!"

Here's a great name for a store selling old things — The DEN OF ANTIQUITY.

★ ★ ★

Heirlooms — when they're yours they're antiques, when they belong to someone else they're simply junk.

★ ★ ★

An antique by any other name would never cost as much.

Ye Olde Shop

Genuine
Imitation
Antiques

"I know this is an antique shop," complained the manager to the owner, "but I don't see why I have to keep working at my old salary!"

A dealer walked into an antique shop and bought an old commode. He got it for a small deposit.

Antique — something you really can't use at a price you really can't afford.

An antique vase may not be as old as it's cracked up to be.

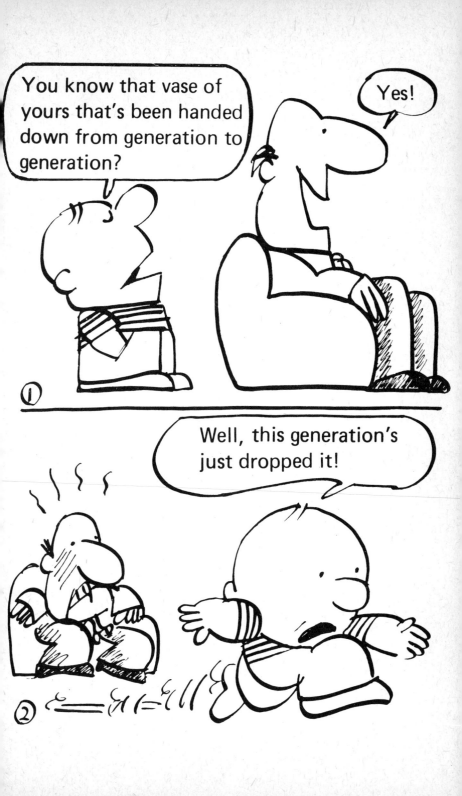

Antique crystal —— that's what you call glass when you're selling.

★ ★ ★

The 17th-century antiques my wife buys at auctions are keeping me baroque!

Antique auction — a place where you get something for nodding.

If this isn't a Stradivarius, I've been robbed of $110.

Jack Benny

Did you hear about the thief who robbed the music store and ran off with the lute?

A Roman penny recently sold at an antique auction for £5,000. I've heard of inflation, but that is ridiculous!

At a New Year's Eve dinner for antique dealers, everybody stood up at midnight and sang, "Should old and quaint things be forgot . . ."